A partnership between American Library Association
and FINRA Investor Education Foundation

FINRA is proud to support the American Library Association

A TEEN GUIDE TO INVESTING
A Dividend Stock Strategy FOR TEENS
TAMMY GAGNE
Mitchell Lane
PUBLISHERS

Disclaimer: Mitchell Lane Publishers is not a securities advisor. The views here belong solely to the author and should not be used or considered as investment advice. Individuals must determine the suitability for their own situation and perform their own due diligence before making any investment. The publisher will not be liable for the results of any investments.

Printing 1 2 3 4 5 6 7 8 9

Library of Congress
Cataloging-in-Publication Data
Gagne, Tammy.
A dividend stock strategy for teens / by Tammy Gagne.
pages cm.—(A teen guide to investing)
Includes bibliographical references and index.
Audience: Grade 7 to 8.
ISBN 978-1-61228-426-2 (library bound)
1. Investments--Juvenile literature. 2. Stocks—Juvenile literature. 3. Finance, Personal—Juvenile literature. I. Title.
HG4521.G175 2014
332.63'22—dc23

2013012289

eBook ISBN: 9781612284880

PLB

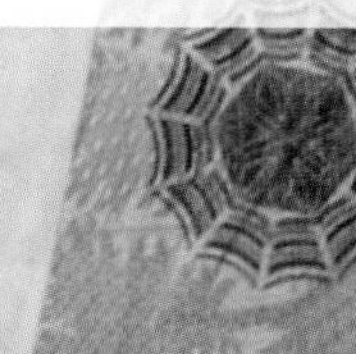

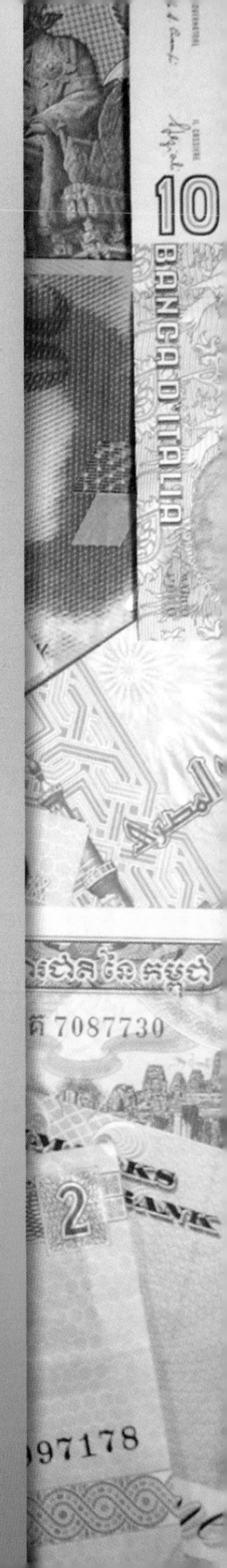

Contents

Investing your money in the stock market comes with some risks. If you pick the right stocks, though, your money can grow very quickly.

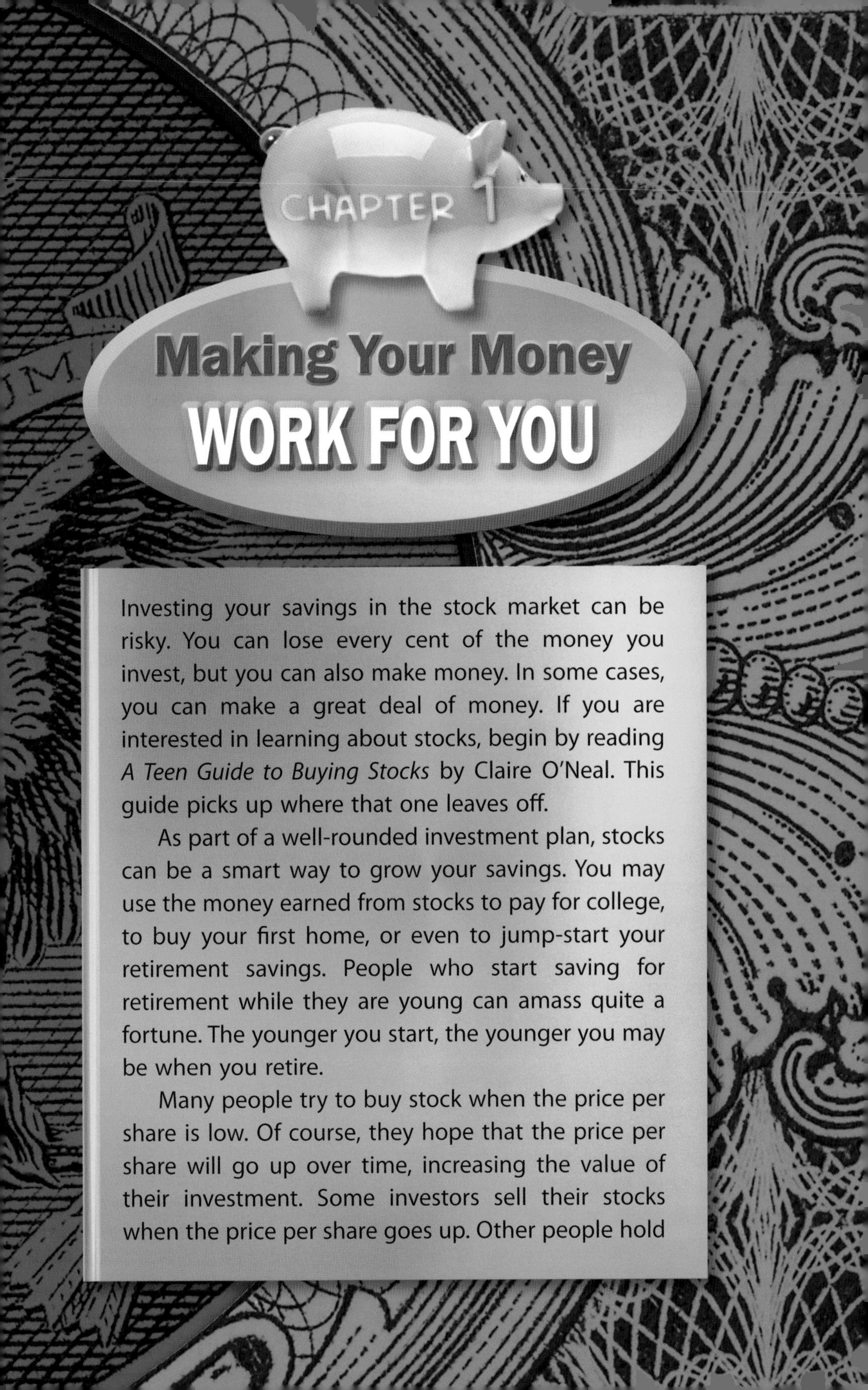

CHAPTER 1

Making Your Money WORK FOR YOU

Investing your savings in the stock market can be risky. You can lose every cent of the money you invest, but you can also make money. In some cases, you can make a great deal of money. If you are interested in learning about stocks, begin by reading *A Teen Guide to Buying Stocks* by Claire O'Neal. This guide picks up where that one leaves off.

As part of a well-rounded investment plan, stocks can be a smart way to grow your savings. You may use the money earned from stocks to pay for college, to buy your first home, or even to jump-start your retirement savings. People who start saving for retirement while they are young can amass quite a fortune. The younger you start, the younger you may be when you retire.

Many people try to buy stock when the price per share is low. Of course, they hope that the price per share will go up over time, increasing the value of their investment. Some investors sell their stocks when the price per share goes up. Other people hold onto stocks even when the price rises. No one knows for sure how much the price of any stock will rise or fall in the future. This uncertainty is the reason that stocks are risky investments. The more you learn about a particular company, though, the better idea you'll have about its chance of succeeding. If you are going to sell, you want to sell high. Selling isn't the only way to make money from stock, however.

You can also use stocks as a way to collect a regular paycheck. Many companies pay dividends to stockholders. The more money you invest and the better the company does, the higher these payments will be. Most dividends are paid quarterly (every three months), but some companies pay them monthly or annually instead.

If your goal is earning dividends, your strategy will not be focused on buying low and selling high. Certainly you want to make as much money as you can from your dividends. Instead of making a large amount of money all at once, though, you want to create a steady income from your stocks. For this reason, you won't be doing quite as much gambling. There is no such thing as a risk-free stock, but some stocks are far less risky than others.

Companies that have proven track records in their fields are most attractive to dividend investors. Ideally, these should be companies that have offered stock to the public for a long period of time as well. Do your homework, so you know how well the stock has performed over its history. Stocks that have gradually increased in value over time show that a company is stable, but growing. This doesn't mean that the price per share has never gone down. Nearly all stocks go through at least some ups and downs, but the safest companies show growth over time.

Stocks that increase in value quickly are known as growth stocks. Usually these companies are expanding and are expected to see rapidly increasing profits or income. These are the investments that people want to buy low and sell high. They may pay low dividends, or may not pay dividends at all, because management would prefer to reinvest profits back into the company. While this arrangement may seem like a

You may have heard the term *nest egg* in relation to stocks and other investments. Creating a nest egg (or savings for the future) while you are young is the best way to make sure you will have enough money as you get older. Buying an income stock today—and holding onto it for many years while it grows—is one way to create a sizeable nest egg for retirement.

bad deal for the stockholders, the goal is to make the company stronger. This could mean that the company is spending that money to develop new technologies, add locations, or hire more staff to serve their customers. If these changes help the company to earn even more money in the long run, its stock is likely to rise in value. Not everyone likes the idea of buying stock that doesn't pay dividends, though. If you want to earn dividends, make sure that the stock you buy is from a company that offers these regular payments.

Large, established companies with stable profits are more likely to pay dividends than those that are still growing. Dividend investments may not seem as exciting as growth stocks. Owning growth stocks can be a bit like being on a roller coaster ride. One day the price may go way up; the next it might fall to below its starting price. It might even

Owning growth stocks can be full of extreme ups and downs. This may sound exciting, but there is nothing fun about losing money. After a big loss, a stock can take a while to climb back up to its original price per share. Some stocks never fully recover from a severe drop in value.

go up and down many times. You won't see as much change in the day-to-day value of stocks that pay dividends. This doesn't mean that their value won't rise over time, though. In some cases, you may even see a rapid increase in the price per share of a dividend stock.

Just as it is up to a company's management to determine whether to pay dividends, the amount of the dividend that will be paid is also determined by management. Increasing profits could lead to increased dividends, but a weak economy could cause a company to cut them. Most companies try to increase or at least maintain their dividends to meet their stockholders' expectations. A drop in the dividend amount could cause stockholders to sell and the stock value could fall.

INVESTOR TRIVIA

Microsoft, one of the largest companies in the world today, went into business in 1975, and became a publicly traded company in 1986. It didn't offer a single dividend to its shareholders, however, until 2003.

It is important to weigh the risk of investing in a stock against the possible reward. The amount of money you earn in dividends each year compared to how much money you invested in a stock is called the yield. Buying stock in a company paying dividends with a 5 percent yield may very well be worth the risk. If a company pays dividends with only a 1 percent yield, though, it may be wiser to put your money elsewhere. Government bonds, for instance, may offer you an interest rate higher than 1 percent. Even if a bond's interest rate is the same as the yield of the stock, your money is probably safer in the bond. Only you can decide if a stock's potential reward is great enough to justify the risk.

Dividend stocks aren't the only choice for long-term investing. In order for the risk of a stock to be worthwhile, you must consider the yield. If the yield is low, you may be able to make the same amount of money by investing your cash in a savings bond instead. And that bond is most likely a safer investment.

The first big expense you will encounter as an adult is college. Saving for education now can reduce (or even eliminate) your need for a student loan down the road.

INVESTOR TRIVIA

Caterpillar Corporation, a company that makes machinery and engines, made $5 billion in profits in 2011. It gave 25 percent, or $1.2 billion, to its shareholders in the form of dividends.

To figure out the yield of a certain stock, you must first find the dividend amount. Let's say that a company's stock is currently priced at $100 per share. Now let's say that the dividends paid by the company in the last year totaled $3 per share. To calculate the yield, you would divide the amount of the annual dividend ($3) by the share price ($100). In this case, the yield is 0.03, or 3 percent.

Once you own a stock, you can also use this method for figuring out your actual annual yield. Just divide the amount of your total dividends for that year by the total value of your stock. If you owned exactly 10 shares in that same stock (10 shares at $100 per share = $1,000) and received a total of $30 in dividends, you would divide $30 by $1,000. The result is the same: 3 percent.

Unfortunately, there is no way to know whether a company will continue to pay the same yield in the future. It may pay the same, it may pay more, or it may pay less. This is where the risk comes in. Doing research can help you keep your risk as low as possible, but you cannot completely eliminate the risk. How a company has done in the past is no guarantee of how it will do in the future.

The most important thing to remember is that you should only invest money that you can afford to lose in the stock market. If you need the money for college, for example, you shouldn't invest it all in stocks. If your parents have already set aside money for your education, however, you may decide to invest money that you inherit from a grandparent or other relative. You may also want to invest money that you make from a part-time job.

Don't let the hectic nature of stock trading rush you into making big decisions. Always think things through before buying or selling stock.

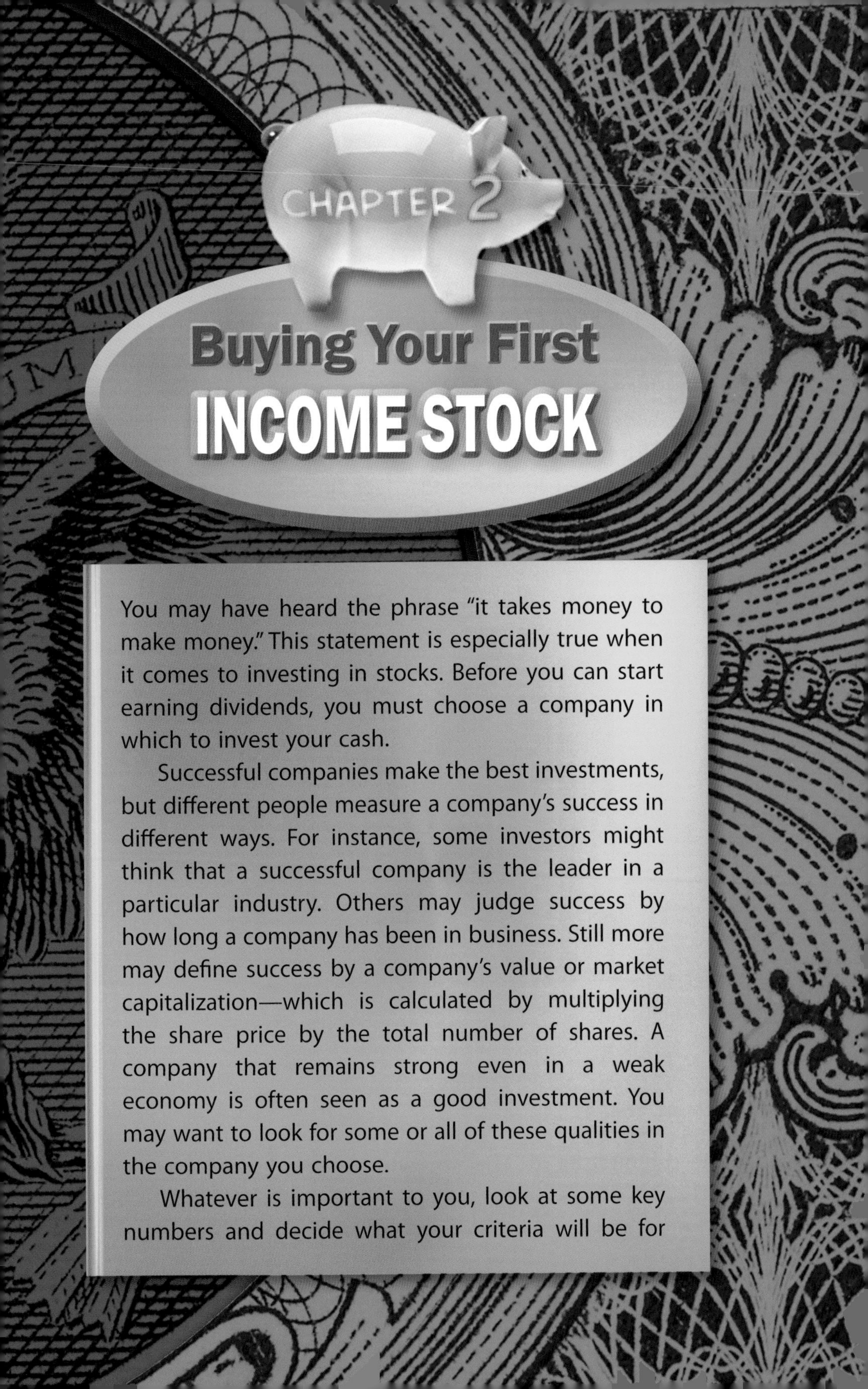

CHAPTER 2

Buying Your First INCOME STOCK

You may have heard the phrase "it takes money to make money." This statement is especially true when it comes to investing in stocks. Before you can start earning dividends, you must choose a company in which to invest your cash.

Successful companies make the best investments, but different people measure a company's success in different ways. For instance, some investors might think that a successful company is the leader in a particular industry. Others may judge success by how long a company has been in business. Still more may define success by a company's value or market capitalization—which is calculated by multiplying the share price by the total number of shares. A company that remains strong even in a weak economy is often seen as a good investment. You may want to look for some or all of these qualities in the company you choose.

Whatever is important to you, look at some key numbers and decide what your criteria will be for investing. You will want to look for a good yield, but don't choose a financially risky company just because it offers a high yield. If a yield seems much higher than others in the industry, be sure to check the financial statements carefully (see *A Teen Guide to Buying Stocks* for a detailed explanation of financial statements). You can also check a stock's financial stability rating with an independent guide like Morningstar.

The dividend yield is one of the most important numbers that you'll be considering, and it's also important to note whether a company has regularly increased its dividends over time. Company X offering a 3 percent yield today could be a better investment in the long run than

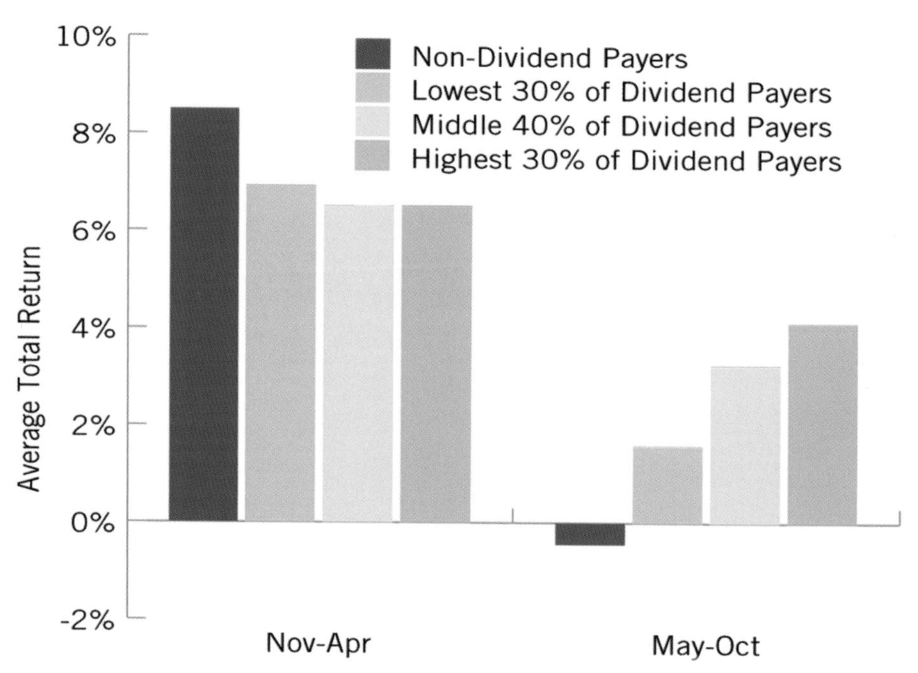

From 04.30.27 through 10.31.11.

While the months of May to October have been historically poor months for stocks, those that pay dividends tend to fare better in these months than non-dividend payers.

Company Y offering a 4 percent yield—if X is consistently increasing dividends. For example, let's say that you invest in ten shares of each company at $100 each. In your first year, X will pay you back $3 per share or $30, versus Y's $4 per share or $40. But what if in five years X's dividend has increased to $7 per share, but Y's is still $4 per share? Now you are making $70 per year or a 7 percent return on your investment in X, but still getting 4 percent from Y. In addition, stock prices often increase when dividends increase, so your investment in X could be worth even more over time.

Lists are available of stocks that have continually increased dividends over time. Stocks on the S&P 500 Dividend Aristocrats have increased their dividends every year for the last twenty-five years; Mergent's Dividend Achievers stocks have increased their dividends consistently for at least ten years.

If you're looking to collect a regular paycheck from your stocks, you may also want to consider the dates that a stock's dividends have been paid in the past. Some investors like to balance their investments so they are receiving checks at least once or twice a month.

In addition to a company's dividend yield, another figure to look for is the return on equity (ROE). Equity is the amount left from the company's total assets (like cash, equipment, or land) after you subtract the liabilities, or debt. Return on equity is simply a measure of how much profit a company makes each year for every dollar that is invested. A 15 percent ROE indicates that a company earned $15 of profit for every $100 that stockholders have invested. You can calculate the return on equity on your own if you have two numbers: the amount of the company's net income and shareholders' equity. The word "net" simply means the amount that's left over after all deductions have been made. To find the ROE, divide the net income by the shareholders' equity. You can find this information on a company's income statement and balance sheet. Consider the ROE for the past several years, and compare it to others in the same industry. Some investors look for this number to be at a certain minimum, for example 10 percent or more.

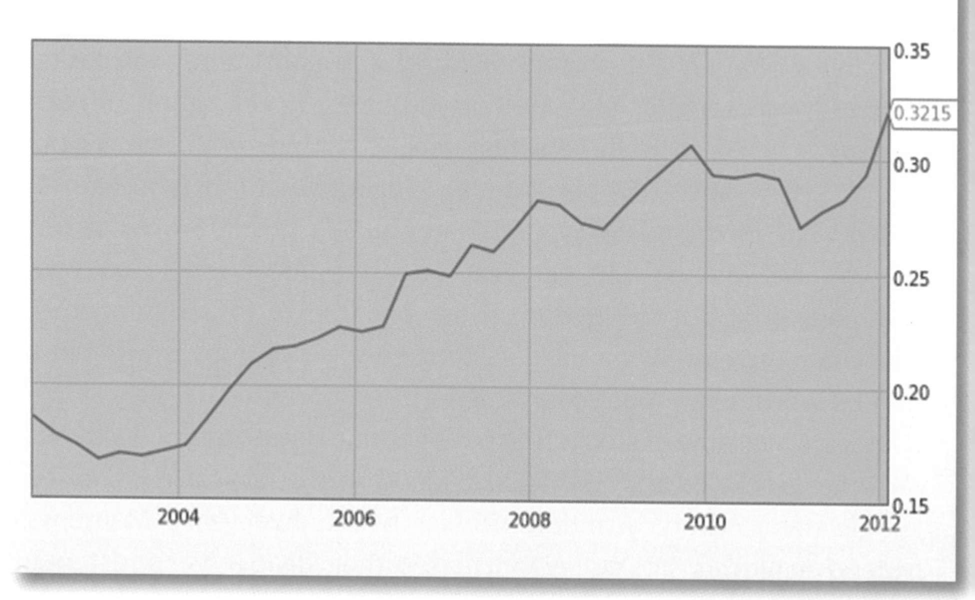

Walmart's payout ratio has gone up and down several times in the last few years. Although this important number has risen steadily, it is still at a level that most experts consider safe. In 2012, Walmart kept 67.85 percent of its profits, which is a significant amount cash to help it weather future financial storms.

Earnings per share (EPS) is a similar measure of profitability. But this number measures how much profit a company made for each share of stock. Consider a company's payout ratio as well—how much of their profit are they paying out in dividends? While it's great to receive as much profit as possible from a company that you invest in, remember that if a company pays out too much of its cash, it might not have

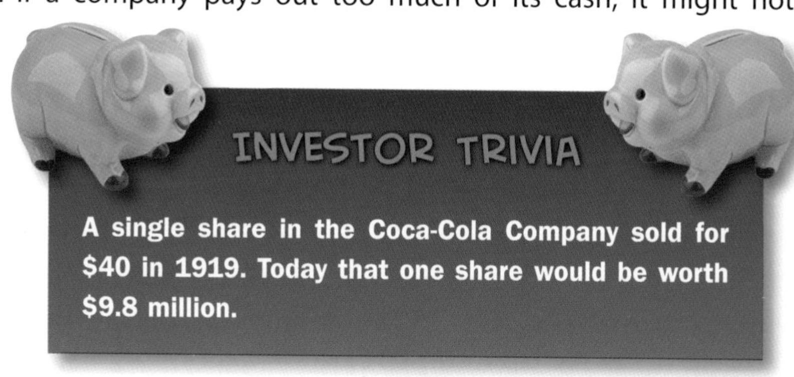

enough left to make it through unexpected difficult times. Many experts recommend stocks with a payout ratio of less than 60 to 80 percent.

Choosing your first stock can be a little overwhelming. To make the process less stressful, take your time. Narrow your choices down to a few different companies, then compare their minimum investment amounts, dividend yields, share prices, earnings per share, and return on equity. You may also want to talk to your parents about which companies they think are the best options. You will need one of them to make the actual purchase with you if you are younger than eighteen years old.

Once you are ready to make your stock purchase, you must decide whether you want to use a broker or purchase your stock directly from

Stockbrokers can offer new investors much knowledge and guidance about the stock market. You must pay for their services, though. It is also important to remember that brokers cannot guarantee that a particular stock will succeed.

the company. Dealing with a broker has changed a lot over the last couple of decades. Online brokerage firms have made purchasing stock easier. Many online firms charge very low fees for stock purchases. Having an online brokerage account also makes managing your investments a simpler matter. Still, you may want to consider buying direct. Brokers make money by charging investors commissions on stock purchases. Not having to pay a commission means more of your money goes directly into the investment.

Hundreds of companies offer direct stock purchase plans (DSPPs), sometimes called direct investment programs (DIPs). If you are

Buying stocks online has never been easier. It is important to do some research before making a purchase, though. You have many choices when it comes to online brokers. You can even buy certain stocks online directly from the companies themselves.

INVESTOR TRIVIA

More than one hundred companies allow DRP investors to buy additional shares at a discount. Investors may save between 3 and 10 percent from the market share price.

interested in a particular company, you can visit its website to find out if it offers a DSPP. Just because you are buying direct, though, doesn't mean you won't have to pay any fees at all. Some companies charge a setup fee, a purchase fee each time more stock is purchased, and fees for selling stock. These fees are often less than those of many brokerage firms, however.

Each company has its own minimum investment amount for stock purchases. Some companies require a minimum stock purchase of $50; others have minimums of $500 or more. Many companies will waive this fee if you are willing to commit to a monthly purchase plan until you reach the minimum amount. A company with a minimum purchase amount of $500, for example, will usually allow new investors to purchase stock if they agree to pay $50 per month for ten months. When the ten months have passed, you can then decide if you want to keep investing the $50 each month or stop.

The money for DSPPs is usually withdrawn directly from the investor's bank account. The deduction will be made on the same day every month. You just need to make sure that the money to pay for the stock is in the account before that time. Some companies will allow you to pay by check, but many charge an additional fee if you choose to use this type of payment.

You can also purchase stock through one of many different online organizations. First Share, Money Paper, and ShareBuilder are just a few of these resources that help new investors get started. These middlemen

Many investment organizations use social media to communicate with investors. If you have a question, post it on the organization's Facebook or Twitter page. You can also learn a lot by reading questions that have already been asked and answered on these sites.

aren't stockbrokers, but they will charge a certain amount for their services. You won't pay them directly, but rather pay slightly higher fees when buying stock through their websites. In most cases, you will do better by buying your stock directly from the company you choose, but be sure to compare all the fees involved with each option.

Once you have purchased stock in a company, you can start earning dividends. You will then have to decide what you want to do with your dividends. If your initial investment is a small one, your dividends won't add up to much in the beginning. This doesn't mean that your dividends don't have value. Whatever the size of your investment, you may decide that the best way to grow your investment is by using your dividends to buy more stock.

Most companies that offer dividends make it easy for their stockholders to buy more stock with their dividends. A dividend reinvestment program (DRP or DRIP) allows you to roll your dividends into additional stock purchases. Your dividends then begin compounding, or producing earnings from previous dividends.

Once you sign up for a DRP, you won't have to do a thing to make these buys. They will occur automatically whenever dividends are paid. Your monthly or quarterly dividend payment may only be enough to purchase a fraction of a share, but over time these partial shares can add up. The longer you reinvest your dividends, the more stock you will accumulate.

If you want to start a DRP, but the company doesn't offer a direct stock purchase plan, you can work around this challenge. Simply purchase your first share (or however many shares you must buy to meet the minimum purchase amount) through a broker. Once you own at least one share, you can then ask the broker to issue you a stock certificate (the broker may charge a fee for this service). You can then provide a copy of this document to the company's shareholder services department to set up your DRP.

Most DRPs offer investors the opportunity to make optional cash payments (OCPs) with low minimum amounts. Perhaps your favorite aunt sends you $25 every year on your birthday. If so, you can easily use this money to make an OCP. Optional cash payments are another way to increase both your number of shares and the amount of your dividends.

Many brokers will now set up a DRP for their clients. Bear in mind that there is a catch to going this route. If you want to buy additional stock through an OCP, you will have to pay a commission on that purchase. Whenever possible, it is better to use the money that would go to a commission towards your stock purchase instead.

Be sure not to put all your eggs in one basket—that is, to invest all your money in a single place.

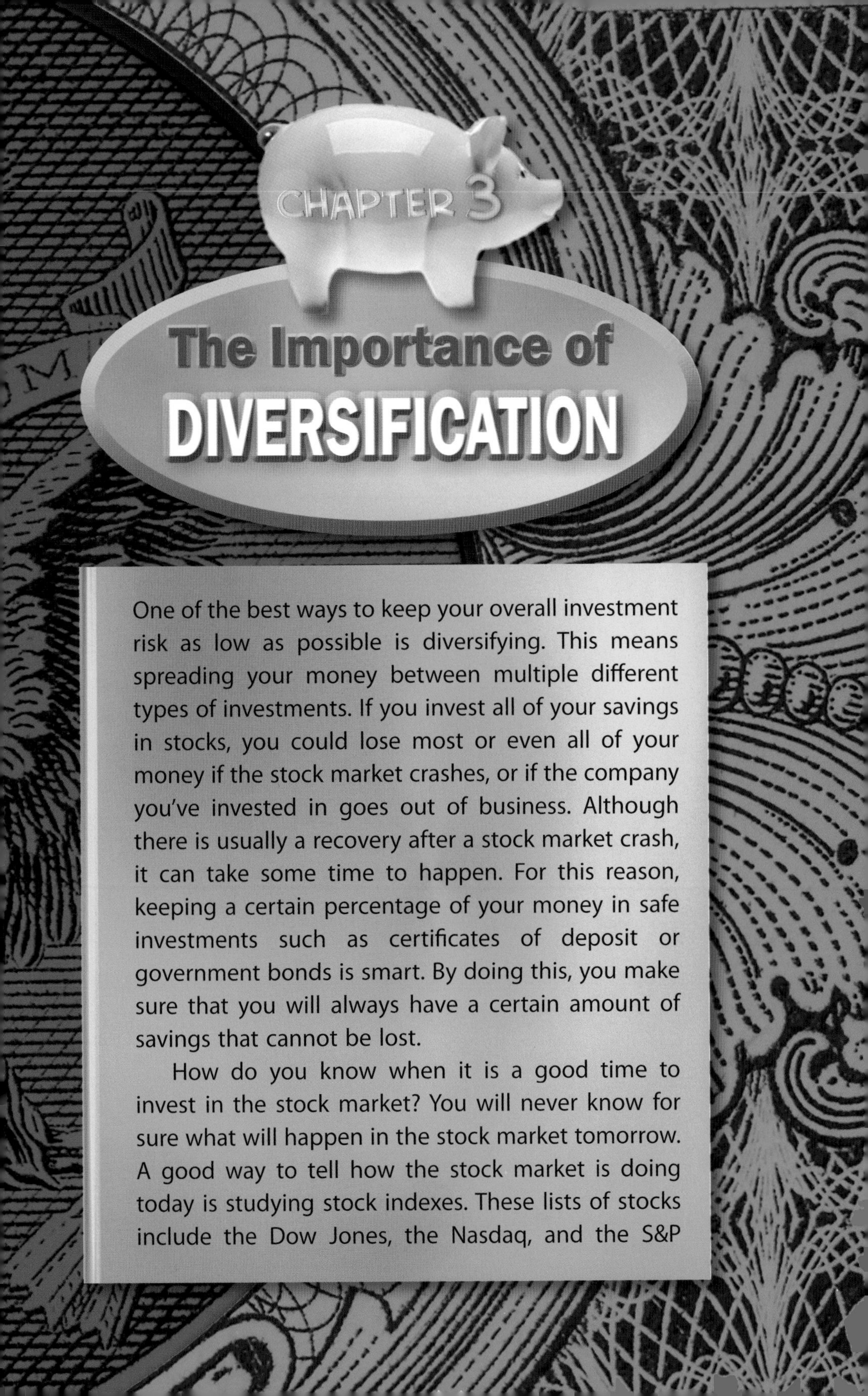

CHAPTER 3

The Importance of DIVERSIFICATION

One of the best ways to keep your overall investment risk as low as possible is diversifying. This means spreading your money between multiple different types of investments. If you invest all of your savings in stocks, you could lose most or even all of your money if the stock market crashes, or if the company you've invested in goes out of business. Although there is usually a recovery after a stock market crash, it can take some time to happen. For this reason, keeping a certain percentage of your money in safe investments such as certificates of deposit or government bonds is smart. By doing this, you make sure that you will always have a certain amount of savings that cannot be lost.

How do you know when it is a good time to invest in the stock market? You will never know for sure what will happen in the stock market tomorrow. A good way to tell how the stock market is doing today is studying stock indexes. These lists of stocks include the Dow Jones, the Nasdaq, and the S&P

With so many options to choose from, investing in stocks can be overwhelming. But by diversifying your investments among different stocks and different types of investments, you can minimize your risk.

500. If you watch the news, you have probably heard reporters talk about the Dow Jones Industrial Average. This number is a weighted average value of thirty of the biggest stocks available today. When a reporter says that the Dow has risen by twenty-five points, he or she means that the cost of buying these stocks today is $25 more expensive than the cost of buying them yesterday. Likewise, a loss of twenty-five points means that the stocks are $25 less expensive than they were at the close of business the previous day. Many investors will wait to purchase stocks when these indexes are low, hoping to buy a solid stock at a discounted price.

You cannot rely on the Dow or any other index to tell you how a specific stock is doing. You can, however, use these indexes to get an idea of how the overall market is performing. If you are thinking about buying stock in a specific company, watch its progress along with the companies on the Dow over a period of time. If the Dow is doing well while your company is rising in value, it could be a sign that the company is a smart pick. If your company continues rising even when the Dow falls a bit, it could be an even better sign that it is a good investment choice. If your company is falling as the Dow stocks are rising, however, be sure to find out why and use that information when you consider your purchase. If your stock is doing badly when other stocks are doing well, what will happen to your investment if the market crashes?

INVESTOR TRIVIA

In 2012, 429 companies on the S&P 500 raised their dividends. This was a 35 percent increase from the previous year.

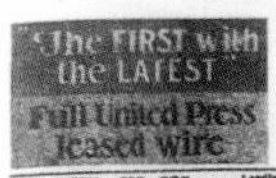
The FIRST with the LATEST
Full United Press Leased Wire

People's Paper · Orange County
Santa Ana Daily Evening Register

FINAL EDITION

VOL. XXIV. NO. 285. SANTA ANA, CALIFORNIA, MONDAY, OCTOBER 28, 1929 20 PAGES 3c Per Copy. 65c Per Month

BILLIONS LOST AS STOCKS CRASH

Pantages In Jail Awaits Sentence To State Prison

SENATE "FARM BLOC" STARTS BATTLE FOR HIGHER TARIFFS

GUILTY SAYS JURY AFTER MANY HOURS

Theater Man Declares He 'Got Raw Deal' and Did Not Even Have Chance

MISS PRINGLE GLAD

In Statement Says Not Sure Whether She Will Continue Her Stage Career

STATE PLANS TO ROUND UP TAX DODGERS

Banks and Corporations to Be Object of Campaign Says Commissioner

Friend Brings Man To Jail On Rum Charge

BINGHAM TAKES EXCEPTION TO SENATE LOBBY

Charges Committee With Unfair Political Tactics During Probe

Alliance Of Two Factions May Win Out

Western Republicans Group With Southern Democrats to Increase Rates

THREE U. S. C. STUDENTS ARE

JURY BELIEVES HER STORY

MAINSTAYS OF MARKET IN PLUNGE

Banking Support Unable to Prevent Break Accompanied by Wild Trading

TICKERS FAR BEHIND

General Electric, U. S. Steel, Other Leading Issues Caught In Crash

During the history of stock markets, several large crashes have occurred. Most stocks recover, even from devastating losses like these, but it can take time. In the case of the 1929 crash, the market continued to lose money for many years before making gains again.

Devastating stock market losses have happened several times throughout history. The crash of 1929 marked the beginning of the Great Depression. Over the next few years, stock values went down more than 80 percent from where they had been in the late 1920s. More than twenty-five years after the stock market crash of 1987, people still talk about October 19 of that year. Now known as Black Monday, this was the day when the Dow Jones Industrial Average sank 508 points. It lost 22.6 percent—the biggest loss ever seen in a single day of trading. The year 2008 also proved to be a bad time for both stocks and the economy in general. On October 15, 2008, the Dow dropped 7.8 percent. All of these losses were eventually recovered, however, as the stock market has continued to increase in value over the long term.

If you want to invest in the stock market, you can't eliminate the risk. You can lower it, however—again, by using diversification. The group of investments in which you invest your money is called your portfolio. Your portfolio may include stocks, bonds, and certificates of deposit (CDs). Your stock portfolio consists of all the shares of stock you hold in different companies. If you invest all your money in a single company, you could lose any or all of it if that stock does poorly. But if you divide your money in half and buy stock in two different companies, you will be in better shape if one of them suffers a loss.

Financial experts disagree about how much an investor should diversify when dividends are the goal. If you are trying to create regular income from dividends, the companies you choose will have many qualities in common. You want to choose companies with proven track records and promising futures. While diversification is important, you don't want to diversify so much that you take a chance on a company that is struggling.

When a company's stock goes down, some people buy as much as they can. The goal of these investors is making a large profit if the company bounces back. They see a stock like this as being a possible bargain. As an income investor, you won't be searching for this type of stock, but instead you will be focused on dividends. When a company starts struggling, dividends are often the first thing to go, as the company needs to use this money to help pay its expenses.

Buying stock after a loss in value can earn you money if the price per share goes back up.

Still, you can and should make a point of buying different stocks. The group of stocks from which you choose

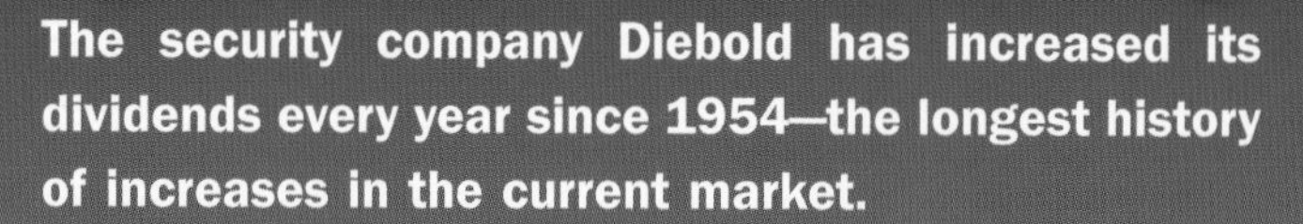

INVESTOR TRIVIA

The security company Diebold has increased its dividends every year since 1954—the longest history of increases in the current market.

may be smaller, but diversification is important. It cannot be said enough: there is no guarantee that any stock will do well. You could invest in one hundred different companies, and all one hundred could go bankrupt. It is unlikely, but possible. At the same time, think about what happens when you spread your money among just ten stocks. If one company's stock does go down in value, you still have nine other stocks that could maintain their share price. Some of them may even go up in value and offset your loss. Likewise, some companies' dividends may decrease while other companies' payments may increase. Many financial experts advise against investing more than 10 percent of your money in stock from a single company.

Although dividends are your main goal, you should also keep an eye on the price per share. If the share price decreases, so does the amount of your investment. You don't need the price per share to increase too quickly, but you don't want it to fall too much either.

This concern leads us to an obvious question: Should you sell your stock if the company starts doing poorly? The answer depends on several factors. First, consider the reason that share price dropped. Is the share price a reflection of a short-term problem that can be overcome, part of an overall market fluctuation, or is it an indication of bigger problems in the company? Is there new information that indicates the company is not as stable as you thought when you first purchased? If so, you may want to sell. You will probably also want to sell if the company has eliminated dividends, since you won't be

Knowing when and if you should sell stock can be tough. Just like buying stock, this decision can be a bit of a gamble.

earning a regular paycheck from this stock anymore. But if you believe the company is still a solid investment, it might be a good time to buy even more stock.

Diversification is about more than buying different stocks. Just as you shouldn't invest all your money in a single company, you also shouldn't put all your money in a single industry. If you do and a problem hits that particular industry, you are likely to suffer losses to your entire stock portfolio. For example, if a new tax is announced on all healthcare companies, the share prices of all of those companies are likely to suffer.

Certainly, you want to research every single company you add to your stock portfolio. You should know as much as possible about each stock you buy. Never buy a stock just for the sake of diversification. It is better to own one stock that you are confident is a good investment than three if two of them are bad risks. Expanding your portfolio will take some time. Go slowly and choose wisely.

For investors who want regular, high-paying dividends, the best choices are often blue-chip stocks.

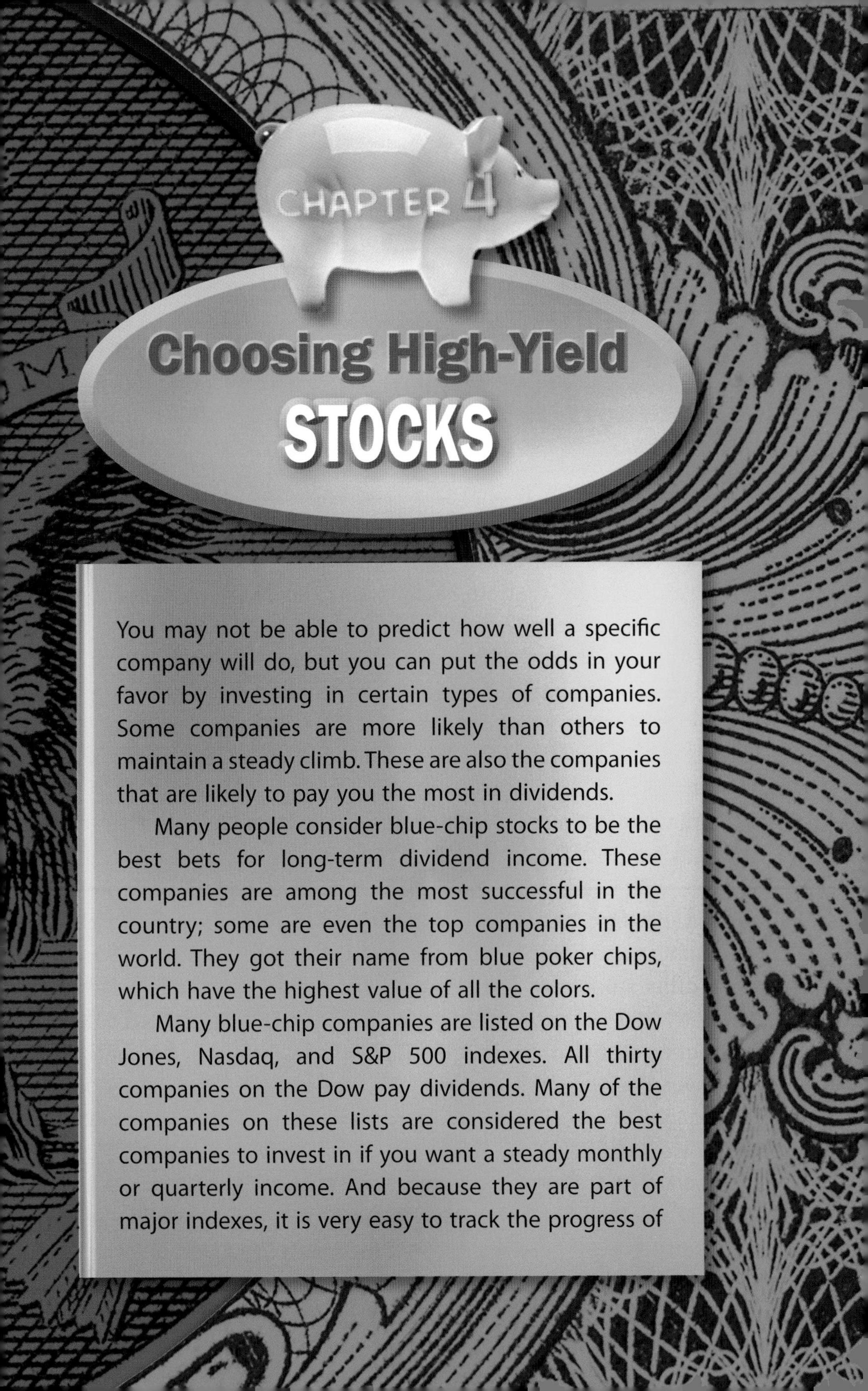

CHAPTER 4

Choosing High-Yield STOCKS

You may not be able to predict how well a specific company will do, but you can put the odds in your favor by investing in certain types of companies. Some companies are more likely than others to maintain a steady climb. These are also the companies that are likely to pay you the most in dividends.

Many people consider blue-chip stocks to be the best bets for long-term dividend income. These companies are among the most successful in the country; some are even the top companies in the world. They got their name from blue poker chips, which have the highest value of all the colors.

Many blue-chip companies are listed on the Dow Jones, Nasdaq, and S&P 500 indexes. All thirty companies on the Dow pay dividends. Many of the companies on these lists are considered the best companies to invest in if you want a steady monthly or quarterly income. And because they are part of major indexes, it is very easy to track the progress of

INVESTOR TRIVIA

Dividend income is taxed at a lower rate than regular income. Most taxpayers will owe the US government 15 percent of their dividends, although low-income investors can keep their dividends tax-free. In 2013, new laws were introduced which charged high-income investors as much as 23.8 percent in dividend taxes. Tax rates are subject to the whim of Congress so there is never any guarantee they will continue to receive favorable tax treatment.

these stocks. Open any financial newspaper or website, and you will be able to check the current price of your stock.

The companies that are likely to pay the highest yields are banks, utilities, real estate investment trusts (REITs), royalty trusts, and master limited partnerships (MLPs). Careful selection is still a must, especially when it comes to banks. Banks that are doing well can pay some of the highest dividends in the stock market. Banks that have done poorly over the last several years, however, have made huge cuts to their dividends.

Utility companies are businesses that provide essential services such as electricity, gas, and water. Even when the economy is bad, people still need these services. For this reason, utility companies usually perform better than many other companies, even in difficult economic conditions. Utility stocks also tend to pay higher dividends than other stocks.

Real estate investment trusts work very much like other companies that offer stock to the public. REITs deal specifically in real estate, however. They buy, sell, and manage various types of property or even mortgages. You might think of these companies as large-scale landlords. REITs were first formed when the Real Estate Investment Trust Act passed in 1960. The act offered these companies certain tax breaks. One of the conditions of qualifying for REIT status is that the company must dispense 90 percent of its net income to its shareholders.

Even if you don't have enough money to buy real estate of your own, you may be able to invest in a real estate investment trust (REIT). Think of this investment as owning shares of a piece of property, or many different properties. REITs offer some of the best yields available today.

Although a few REITs offer direct stock purchase plans, many do not, so shares of their companies must be bought through a broker. Aside from their high yields, one of the biggest advantages of REITs is their price. Many of them trade for just $10 to $40 a share and offer dividend yields between 3 and 12 percent.

Royalty trusts are similar to REITs, but these companies deal specifically in land that is high in natural energy sources, such as oil. It's easy to see why these investments are good ones right now. The rising costs of coal, oil, and natural gas make royalty trusts profitable investments. Their dividends often pay between 9 and 15 percent. Because royalty trusts pay so much to their investors, though, consider a company's cash flow before investing. If something goes wrong, will the company be able to continue paying such high dividends?

Atlas Pipeline Partners is an example of a master limited partnership (MLP). People who invest in an MLP are called limited partners, not shareholders. They also own units, not shares, in the companies. These companies do not pay dividends, but rather quarterly required distributions (QRDs).

Master limited partnerships also share 90 percent or more of their profits with the people who invest in their companies. Investors in MLPs aren't called shareholders, though. Instead, they are limited partners in the companies. Also, the parts of the company that these limited partners own aren't shares; they are called units.

The government limits the types of companies that can offer MLPs to their investors. You can usually spot an MLP by the letters "LP" at the end of the company's name. Many of these businesses deal in commodities and natural resource materials. A small number of them are money management firms.

Master limited partnerships also don't use the term dividends. Instead, they pay out what they call quarterly required distributions (QRDs). These payments work a lot like dividends, but there is one

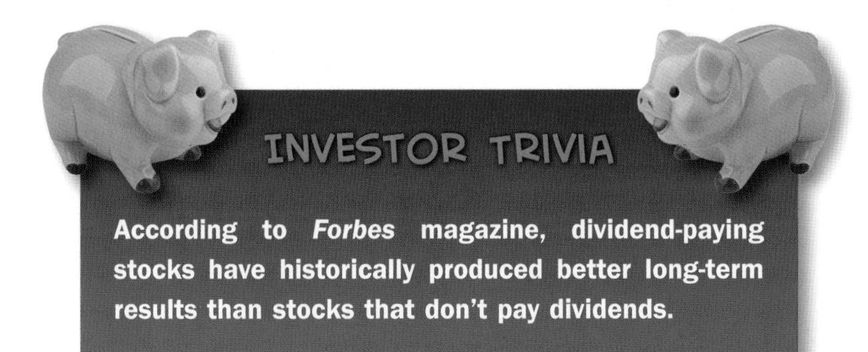

According to *Forbes* magazine, dividend-paying stocks have historically produced better long-term results than stocks that don't pay dividends.

important difference. Master limited partnerships must make these payments to their investors.

The advantage for the companies that qualify as master limited partnerships is that they pay no corporate income taxes. For this reason, MLPs usually offer much higher yields on their QRDs than most stock dividends pay. You also may be able to pay lower taxes when you receive your QRD payments, but taxes could be higher than ordinary capital gains taxes when you sell. You will also need to file more complicated tax forms each year when you invest in an MLP.

Guaranteed payouts and high yields are definite advantages. But these benefits do not erase the risk of investing in any of these companies. In these cases, the risk comes into play when you consider how well a particular company performs. If a company fails, 90 percent of its profits could be nothing at all.

Income stocks should be long-term investments. Ideally, you want to buy stock and keep it for many years. Trading is always an option, of course, and sometimes it must be done to limit losses. In general, though, you want to buy stock in the companies that are most likely to weather any financial storms they may encounter.

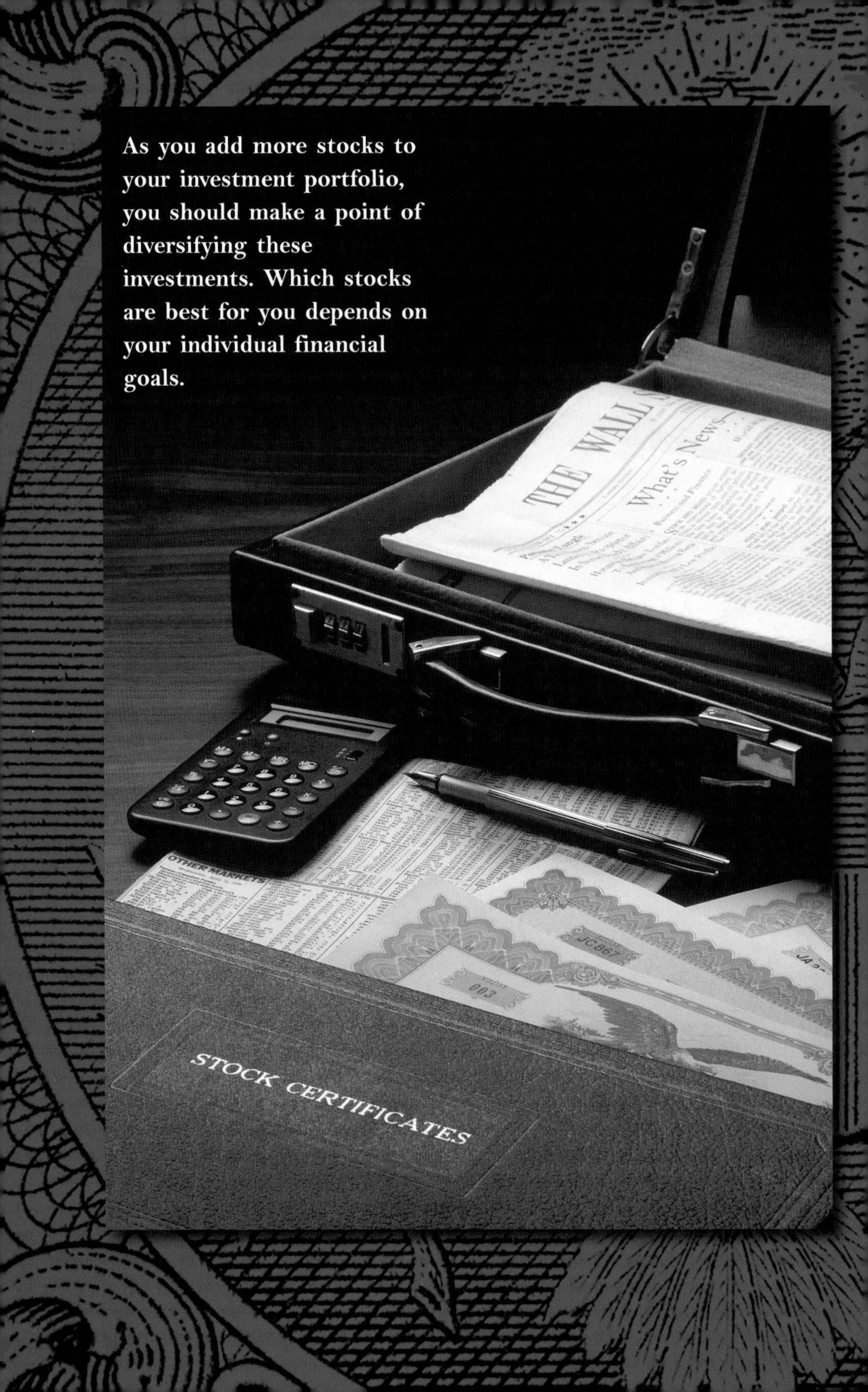

As you add more stocks to your investment portfolio, you should make a point of diversifying these investments. Which stocks are best for you depends on your individual financial goals.

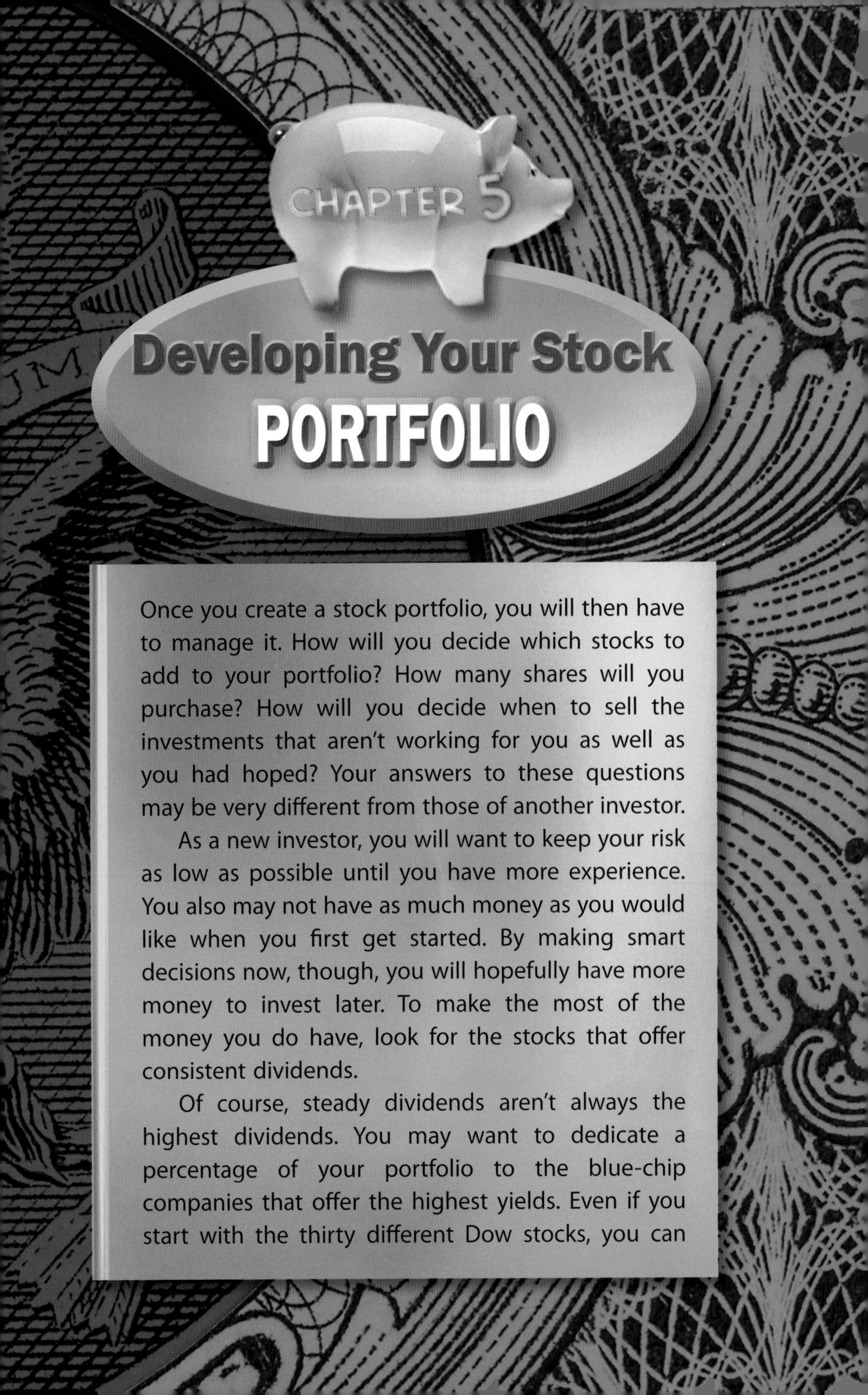

CHAPTER 5

Developing Your Stock PORTFOLIO

Once you create a stock portfolio, you will then have to manage it. How will you decide which stocks to add to your portfolio? How many shares will you purchase? How will you decide when to sell the investments that aren't working for you as well as you had hoped? Your answers to these questions may be very different from those of another investor.

As a new investor, you will want to keep your risk as low as possible until you have more experience. You also may not have as much money as you would like when you first get started. By making smart decisions now, though, you will hopefully have more money to invest later. To make the most of the money you do have, look for the stocks that offer consistent dividends.

Of course, steady dividends aren't always the highest dividends. You may want to dedicate a percentage of your portfolio to the blue-chip companies that offer the highest yields. Even if you start with the thirty different Dow stocks, you can easily identify the five or ten companies that pay the most in dividends. Some investors buy only these stocks. In a year's time they may even sell any stocks that have dropped off this list, replacing them with the companies that have taken their place in the top ten. You should never buy a stock based on yield alone, though. Be sure to research a company's history, finances, and management thoroughly before you invest.

Let's say you have $1,000 to start your stock portfolio. You might decide to divide your money equally between two stocks, buying $500 worth of shares in each company. Another option would be putting more money into the stock that pays the higher yield. Perhaps you would invest $750 in that stock and $250 in the other. You could even choose three stocks. In this case you could invest $333.33 in each company, or $500 in one and $250 in each of the other two. As long as you satisfy the minimum purchase amounts, you can divide your initial investment any way you choose. As you have more money to invest, you may want to diversify further to reduce your risk.

Even if you have enough money to buy your stock outright, you might still consider paying a monthly amount for a direct stock purchase plan instead. This strategy, called dollar cost averaging, is another way you can reduce your risk. Suppose you buy $500 worth of stock today in a company whose shares are selling for $25 each. Maybe

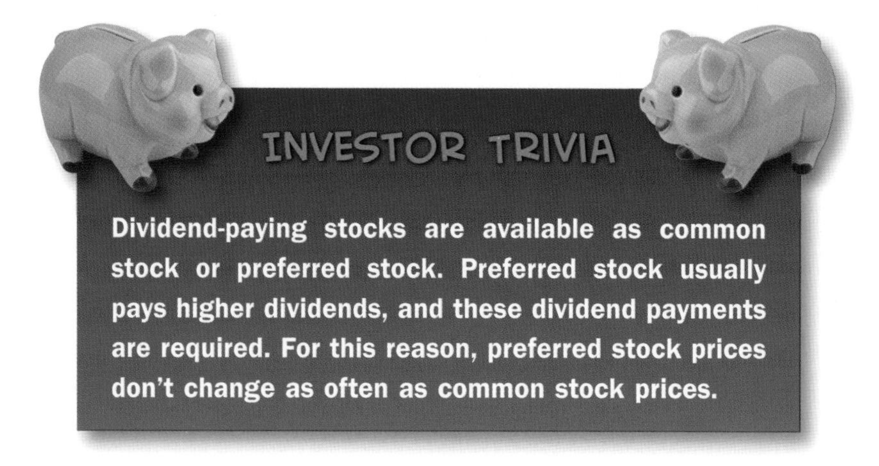

INVESTOR TRIVIA

Dividend-paying stocks are available as common stock or preferred stock. Preferred stock usually pays higher dividends, and these dividend payments are required. For this reason, preferred stock prices don't change as often as common stock prices.

Ideally, you want your stock to rise in value. In some ways, though, a drop in price can end up being a good thing. By taking advantage of dollar cost averaging, you can buy more shares at the lower price. Your investment will increase in value as the price goes back up over time.

you have done your homework and are confident that the stock will pay you regular dividends and also go up in value over the next five years. Now suppose that the stock drops by $5 per share next month, and drops again by another $5 the following month. Your investment may still go up in value over time, but for right now you have lost money, $200 to be exact. If you had invested $50 monthly instead, you would have more cash available to buy more shares when the price dropped. You would have also lost less money when the stock price fell. Of course, if the price had increased as you expected, then your later purchases would have been made at those higher prices.

If you have a part-time job, you may decide to invest in two or three different DSPPs. If you choose companies that have minimum monthly amounts of just $25, these investments would only cost you $75 each month. If you consider how much money you will make back in dividends, your monthly investment is even less. If you want to make even more, you could enroll in the companies' dividend reinvestment programs—an even better way to take advantage of dollar cost averaging.

No matter what your personal dividend stock strategy is, make thorough research a regular part of any stock purchase you make. Once you have chosen a company, read up on it everywhere you can. And don't forget to read about the competition. Listen to what your parents and friends have to say about the company as well, especially if they are customers of the company or another one like it. Sometimes it doesn't take a financial expert to identify a flaw in a particular company. Even companies that were once leaders in their industries can make costly mistakes and end up worthless.

Take for example the story of Eastman Kodak. In 1888, Eastman Kodak introduced a camera that was unlike any camera that had come before it. With the slogan "you press the button, we do the rest," Kodak aimed to make photography accessible to the everyday consumer. Kodak continued to innovate, making cameras easier to use and film

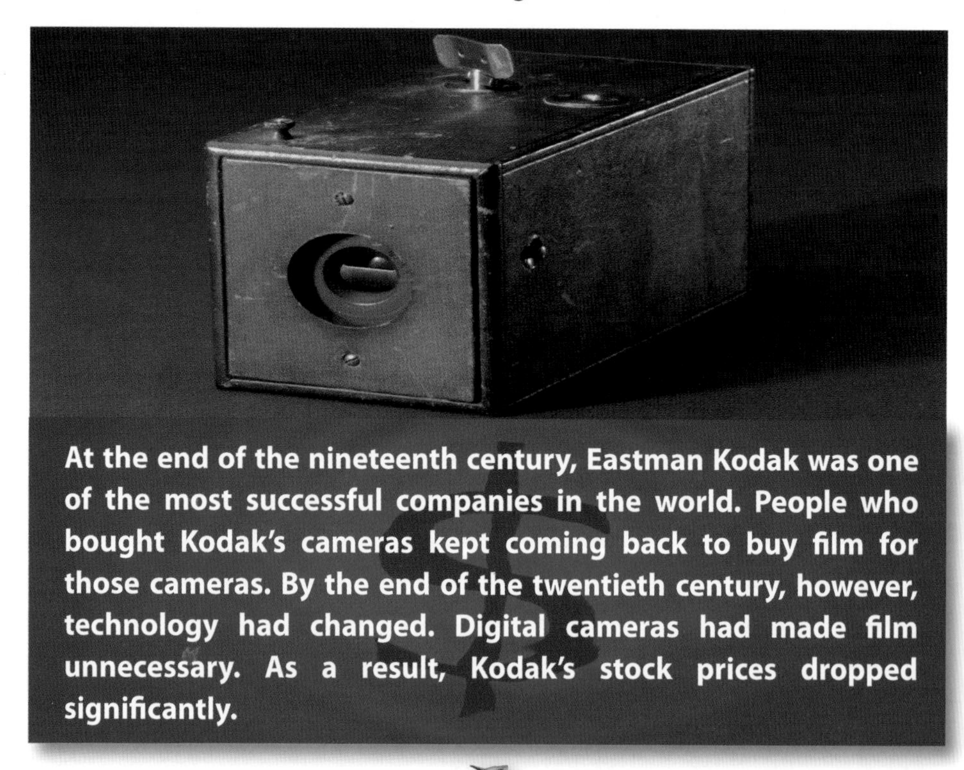

At the end of the nineteenth century, Eastman Kodak was one of the most successful companies in the world. People who bought Kodak's cameras kept coming back to buy film for those cameras. By the end of the twentieth century, however, technology had changed. Digital cameras had made film unnecessary. As a result, Kodak's stock prices dropped significantly.

The biggest disadvantage to buying your stock through a DSPP instead of a broker is that you have no control over the share price on the day your stock is purchased. Sales made with DSPPs can take up to two weeks to go through. Whatever the price per share is on the day the deal is finalized is the price you will pay.

easier to develop. By 1930, Eastman Kodak was a blue-chip company listed on the Dow Jones Industrial Average. Through the early 1990s, the stock paid steadily increasing dividends.

Kodak's business model focused on selling film, not cameras. Film was cheaper to produce, more profitable, and consumable—so consumers would purchase it over and over again. Cameras were bought much less often. But the digital age was beginning to take shape, and film was quickly becoming obsolete. The company that once led the industry in innovation was being slowly pushed out of the market by other companies that were making advances with new technology. Some analysts suggest that Kodak's management had become complacent, relying on the company's past success and reputation instead of seeking out new ideas. Meanwhile, competitors continued to make newer and better products.

In 1994, Kodak announced its first dividend cut, keeping additional cash in its bank account to invest in developing digital technology. A new CEO was hired to bring Kodak into the modern age. It seemed that Kodak was keeping pace with the industry, and its stock price climbed to a high of $94.75 in 1997. Unfortunately, Kodak's efforts to change were too little, too late. By 2003, the company was forced to cut dividends again, and in 2004 the stock was removed from the Dow. In 2009, dividends were eliminated completely and share prices sunk to $2.01.

As part of its 2012 bankruptcy filing, Kodak announced a new business structure intended to bring the company and its products into the twenty-first century. It remains to be seen, however, whether Kodak can re-emerge as a successful company once again.

In a rapidly changing world, examples of once-strong companies unable to keep up are easy to find. The recession that began in 2007 highlighted weaknesses in many companies, especially banks. As a result of the financial crisis, Bank of America was forced to cut its annual dividends from $2.24 in 2008 to just $0.04 the following year. Shares that had traded as high as $45.08 in 2008 traded at a low of $2.53 in 2009. Although share prices have increased since then, they have yet to fully recover, and dividends are still low.

Other stocks that were once considered growth stocks have matured into stable dividend stocks. Companies like Microsoft and Intel were on the cutting edge of technology when they were formed. Today, they are household names that many analysts consider to be good investments. But if they don't keep up with their competitors, even these companies could find themselves out of business.

While many people get their advice from experienced analysts, even these "experts" make mistakes. Young people may be at an advantage in picking strong stocks for the future, since they are often more aware of changes that are happening in the industries that they like. Many famous investors recommend "buying what you know"—or building a stock portfolio of companies whose products and services you actually use. As a consumer, you know what you like and what you don't. With a little research, you may be able to identify which companies' plans are likely to be successful in the future, and which ones are beginning to lag behind the times.

Still, it is smart to keep your emotions out of your stock portfolio. Perhaps you would like to own stock in your favorite restaurant or clothing company. If the research supports the idea to invest in this company, there is certainly nothing wrong with doing so, as long as you let the numbers guide your decisions.

2013 DIVIDEND STOCKS TO CONSIDER

Here are just a few of the top dividend stocks for 2013.

Dividend Aristocrats for 2013

Stock	Symbol	Type	Price (April 30, 2013)	Annual Dividend (April 30, 2013)	Yield
AFLAC, Inc.	AFL	Financials	54.44	1.40	2.57%
W.W. Grainger, Inc.	GWW	Industrials	246.47	3.20	1.30%
PPG Industries, Inc.	PPG	Materials	147.14	2.36	1.60%
Sherwin-Williams Co.	SHW	Materials	183.11	2.00	1.09%
Medtronic, Inc.	MDT	Health Care	46.68	1.04	2.23%
The McGraw-Hill Companies, Inc.	MHP	Research Services	54.11	1.12	2.07%
Archer Daniels Midland Co.	ADM	Consumer Staples	33.94	0.76	2.24%
VF Corporation	VFC	Consumer Discretionary	178.22	3.48	1.95%
PepsiCo, Inc.	PEP	Consumer Staples	82.47	2.15	2.60%
Coca-Cola Co.	KO	Consumer Staples	42.33	1.12	2.65%

Dogs of the Dow for 2013

Stock	Symbol	Type	Price (April 30, 2013)	Annual Dividend (April 30, 2013)	Yield (April 30, 2013)
AT&T, Inc.	T	Technology	37.46	1.80	4.81%
Verizon Communications Inc.	VZ	Technology	53.91	2.06	3.82%
Intel Corporation	INTC	Technology	23.95	0.90	3.76%
Merck & Co. Inc.	MRK	Health Care	47.00	1.72	3.66%
General Electric Company	GE	Industrials	22.29	0.76	3.41%
Pfizer Inc.	PFE	Health Care	29.07	0.96	3.30%
E.I. du Pont de Nemours and Company	DD	Materials	54.51	1.72	3.16%
McDonald's Corp.	MCD	Services	102.14	3.08	3.02%
Johnson & Johnson	JNJ	Health Care	85.23	2.44	2.86%
Hewlett-Packard Company	HPQ	Technology	20.60	0.53	2.57%

High Yield Utilities for 2013

Stock	Symbol	Price (April 30, 2013)	Annual Dividend (April 30, 2013)	Yield (April 30, 2013)
Pepco	POM	21.50	1.08	5.02%
Ameren Corp.	AEE	36.25	1.66	4.59%
Integrys Energy	TEG	61.56	2.83	4.6%
Duke Energy	DUK	75.20	3.23	4.3%
TransAlta Corp.	TAC	14.71	1.15	7.83%
Public Serv. Enterprise	PEG	36.61	1.55	4.23%
Hawaiian Elec.	HE	28.30	1.28	4.52%
Southern Company	SO	48.23	1.96	4.06%
Northwestern Corp.	NWE	43.02	1.52	3.53%
New Jersey Resources Corp.	NJR	47.20	1.60	3.39%

Note: These lists are not purchase recommendations. Use them as a starting point to research stocks for your portfolio.

High Yield Bank Stocks for 2013

Stock	Symbol	Price (April 30, 2013)	Annual Dividend (April 30, 2013)	Yield (April 30, 2013)
New York Community Bancorp	NYCB	13.55	1.00	7.38%
First Financial Bancorp	FFBC	15.37	1.12	7.29%
Valley National Bancorp	VLY	8.99	0.65	7.25%
Park National Corp.	PRK	68.38	3.76	5.50%
People's United Financial Inc.	PBCT	13.16	0.65	4.95%
TrustCo Bank Corp. NY	TRST	5.36	0.26	4.93%
United Bankshares Inc.	UBSI	25.31	1.24	4.90%
Univest Corporation of Pennsylvania	UVSP	17.53	0.80	4.56%
Washington Banking Co.	WBCO	13.80	0.60	4.35%
FirstMerit Corporation	FMER	17.13	0.64	3.74%

REITs to Consider for 2013

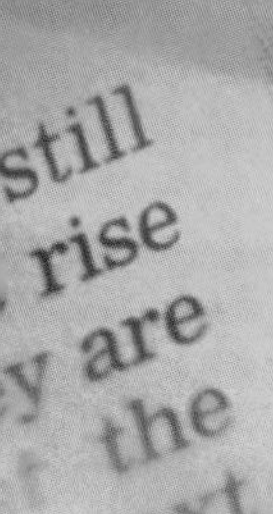

Equity	Symbol	Price (April 30, 2013)	Annual Dividend (April 30, 2013)	Yield (April 30, 2013)
Annaly Capital Management, Inc.	NLY	15.94	1.80	11.29%
Mack-Cali Realty Corp.	CLI	27.77	1.80	6.48%
Hospitality Properties Trust	HPT	29.41	1.88	6.39%
One Liberty Properties, Inc.	OLP	22.94	1.40	6.10%
Corrections Corporation of America	CXW	36.20	2.12	5.86%
The Geo Group, Inc.	GEO	37.45	2.00	5.34%
Lexington Realty Trust	LXP	12.81	0.60	4.68%
WP Carey, Inc.	WPC	70.52	3.28	4.65%
Vornado Realty Trust	VNO	87.56	2.92	3.33%
Cousins Properties, Inc.	CUZ	10.92	0.18	1.65%

MLPs to Consider for 2013

Stock	Symbol	Price (April 30, 2013)	Annual Dividend (April 30, 2013)	Yield (April 30, 2013)
Northern Tier Energy, LP	NTI	26.38	5.08	19.26%
Rhino Resource Partners, LP	RNO	14.58	1.78	12.21%
Navios Maritime Partners, LP	NMM	15.16	1.77	11.69%
LRR Energy, LP	LRE	16.73	1.93	11.52%
QR Energy, LP	QRE	18.26	1.95	10.67%
Capital Product Partners, LP	CPLP	8.90	0.93	10.47%
Natural Resource Partners, LP	NRP	23.88	2.20	9.21%
Breitburn Energy Partners, LP	BBEP	20.45	1.88	9.19%
Legacy Reserves, LP	LGCY	26.68	2.30	8.62%
Crestwood Midstream Partners, LP	CMLP	23.98	2.04	8.51%

Note: These lists are not purchase recommendations. Use them as a starting point to research stocks for your portfolio.

Bamford, Janet. *Street Wise: A Guide for Teen Investors.* Princeton, New Jersey: Bloomberg Press, 2000.
Bateman, Katherine R. *The Young Investor: Projects and Activities for Making Your Money Grow.* Chicago: Chicago Review Press, 2010.
Gardner, David, and Tom Gardner. *The Motley Fool Investment Guide for Teens.* New York: Fireside, 2002.
Karlitz, Gail. *Growing Money: A Complete Investing Guide for Kids.* New York: Price Stern Sloan, 2010.

On the Internet

Dividend.com
http://www.dividend.com/
Morningstar
http://www.morningstar.com/
Teens Guide to Money: "Teens Guide to Investing"
http://www.teensguidetomoney.com/investing/
The Motley Fool: "Dividends & Income"
http://www.fool.com/investing/dividends-income/index.aspx?source=ifltnvsnv0000001

Works Consulted

Brown, Abram. "Coca-Cola Recommends 2-For-1 Stock Split; Shares At 14-Year High." Forbes.com, April 25, 2012.
http://www.forbes.com/sites/abrambrown/2012/04/25/coca-cola-recommends-2-for-1-stock-split-shares-at-14-year-high/
Buckingham, John. "Top 5 Little-Known Reasons to Like Dividend Stocks." Forbes.com, June 15, 2012.
http://www.forbes.com/sites/johnbuckingham/2012/06/15/top-5-little-known-reasons-to-like-dividend-stocks/#
Christ, Ginger. "Number of S&P 500 Members Paying Dividends Highest Since 1999." *Dayton Business Journal,* March 30, 2012.
http://www.bizjournals.com/dayton/print-edition/2012/03/30/number-of-sp-500-members-paying.html?page=all
DRIPInvestor.com. "Buying Stocks Without A Broker Using Dividend Reinvestment Plans."
http://www.dripinvestor.com/FAQ/drip_faq.asp
Kelly, Jason. *The Neatest Little Guide to Stock Market Investing.* New York: Plume, 2007.
Kotter, John. "Barriers to Change: The Real Reason Behind the Kodak Downfall." Forbes.com, May 2, 2012.
http://www.forbes.com/sites/johnkotter/2012/05/02/barriers-to-change-the-real-reason-behind-the-kodak-downfall/
Krantz, Matt. *Investing Online for Dummies.* Hoboken, New Jersey: Wiley Publishing, Inc., 2010.
Mladjenovic, Paul. *Stock Investing for Dummies.* Hoboken, New Jersey: Wiley Publishing, Inc., 2009.
PBS: *The First Measured Century,* "Stock Market Crash."
http://www.pbs.org/fmc/timeline/estockmktcrash.htm
Schlesinger, Jill. "Lessons From the 1987 Stock Market Crash, 25 Years Later." CBS News, October 19, 2012.
http://www.cbsnews.com/8301-505123_162-57534843/lessons-from-the-1987-stock-market-crash-25-years-later/
University of Maine at Augusta: *The Tao of the Dow.* "Counting on Dividends." http://www.uma.edu/counting-on-dividends.html
Weltman, Barbara. "Teach Kids to Diversify Their Investments." FamilyEducation.com.
http://life.familyeducation.com/money-and-kids/investments/48123.html

bankrupt (BANGK-ruhpt): unable to pay one's debts

broker (BROH-ker): a person or company that buys and sells investments on behalf of another person or company in exchange for a commission

cash flow: the amount of money coming in and going out over time

commission (kuh-MISH-uhn): a sum of money paid to a sales agent or broker for his or her services

compound (KOM-pound): to pay interest on the accrued interest as well as on the principal

diversify (dih-VUR-suh-fahy): to spread one's money among different investments or types of investments

dividend (DIV-i-dend): a sum of money paid to shareholders from profits

dollar cost averaging: purchasing an investment in small, regular increments over time to lower risk

earnings per share: the amount of profit a company earns for each outstanding share of stock

economy (ih-KON-uh-mee): the money, jobs, production, and management of resources by a community or country

index (IN-deks): a list of stocks that provide a sample of the overall advancement or decline of the stock market

market capitalization (MAHR-kit kap-ih-tuhl-uh-ZEY-shuhn): the value of a company's total outstanding shares

net income (NET IN-kuhm): the amount of money a company receives from its operations after all expenses are deducted

payout ratio (PEY-out REY-shee-oh): the percentage of net income that a company pays out in dividends to its shareholders

portfolio (pawrt-FOH-lee-oh): the total holdings of an investor

shareholders' equity (SHAIR-hohl-derz EK-wi-tee): a company's assets (such as cash, real estate, or equipment) minus its liabilities, or debt

yield (YEELD): the annual income produced by a financial investment as a percentage of the original investment

Index

About the AUTHOR

Tammy Gagne has authored more than seventy-five books for both adults and children over the last decade. She has been investing for twice this time. In addition to managing her own portfolio, she has taught her teenage son about the details of his investments, enabling him to make some of his own decisions in this area. She believes that young people should know how money works, so their money can work for them instead of vice versa. When young people understand investing and feel in control of their finances, they get excited about money. They also tend to have more of it.